Animal FEET

Contents

Greg Pyers

RIGBY

This is an ape.
It uses its feet to climb.

It holds on to the tree
with its feet.

This is a badger.
It uses its feet to dig.

It digs into the ground
with its **claws**.

This is a bat.
It uses its feet to hang
upside down.

It holds on to the branch with its feet.

This is a blackbird.
It uses its feet to **perch**.

It holds on to the branch
with its feet.

This is an eagle.
It uses its feet to catch fish.

It **snatches** fish from
the water with its **talons**.

This is a turtle.
It uses its feet to swim.

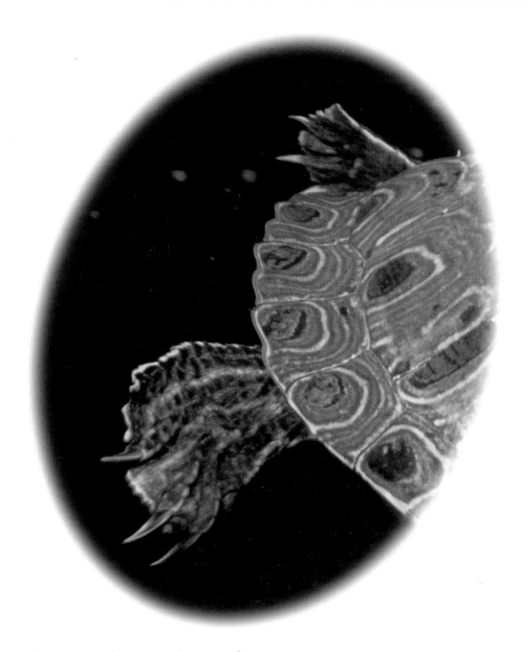

It swims in the water
with its **webbed feet**.

This is a **water bird**.
It uses its feet to walk.

It walks on the **water lilies** with its long toes.

Glossary

claws	the hard, sharp nails on animals' feet
perch	to sit or stand on something for a short time
snatches	grabs something suddenly
talons	hooked claws
water bird	a type of bird that lives near water or marshland
water lilies	a type of plant with large, flat leaves that grows in water
webbed feet	feet that have a piece of skin that joins the toes